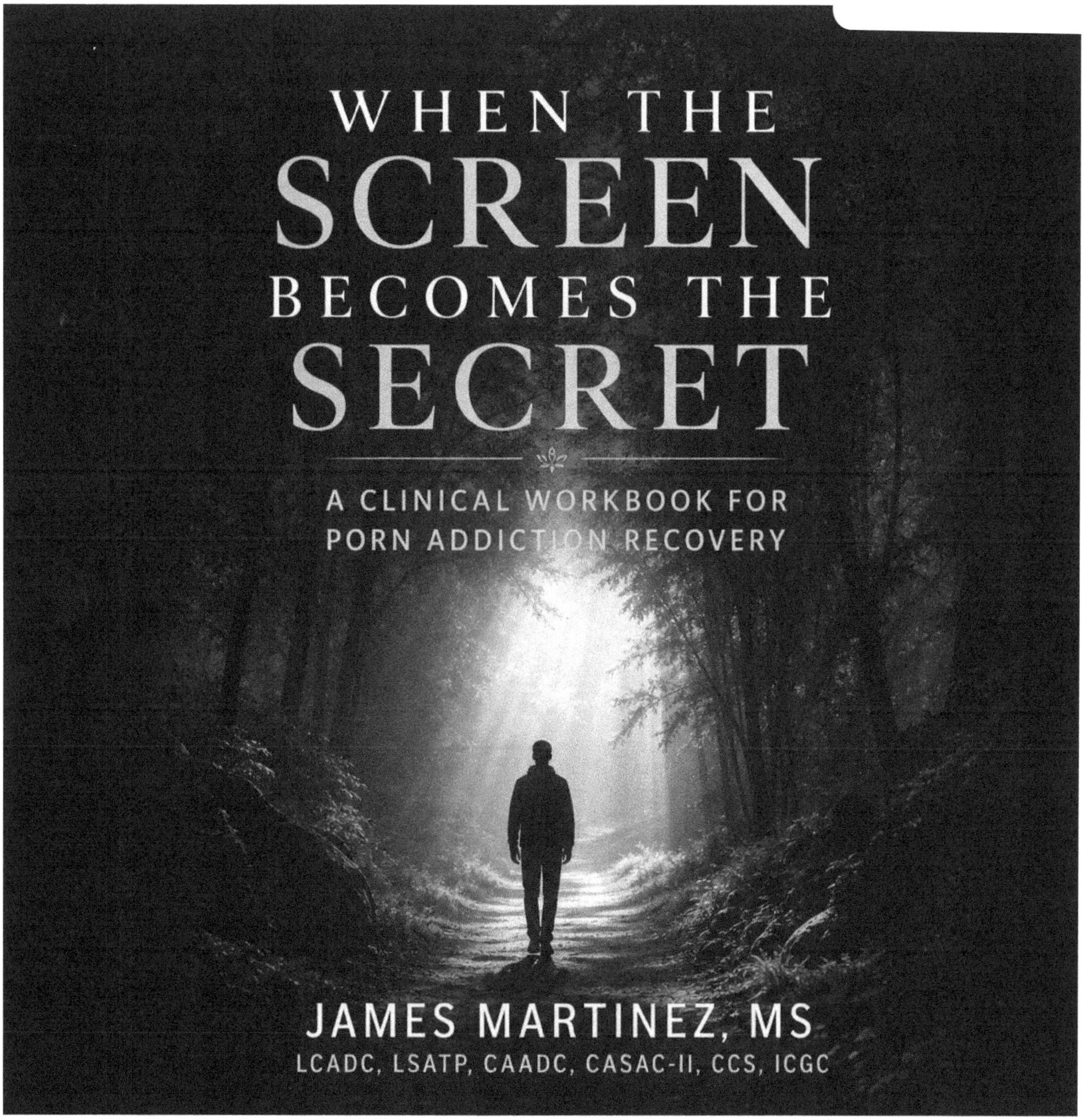
WHEN THE
SCREEN
BECOMES THE
SECRET
A CLINICAL WORKBOOK FOR
PORN ADDICTION RECOVERY
JAMES MARTINEZ, MS
LCADC, LSATP, CAADC, CASAC-II, CCS, ICGC

WHEN THE SCREEN BECOMES THE SECRET

A Clinical Workbook for Porn Addiction Recovery

James Martinez, MS, LCADC, LSATP, CAADC, CASAC-II, CCS, ICGC

Licensed Addiction Therapist

Stress Free Recovery LLC — United States

Printed in the United States of America.

All case examples and vignettes in this workbook are **composite illustrations** created for educational purposes. They do not represent any real individual.

Disclaimer

This workbook is an **educational and therapeutic support tool** designed to assist individuals recovering from compulsive pornography use and Compulsive Sexual Behavior Disorder (CSBD).

It is **not**:

- A substitute for therapy
- A diagnostic tool
- A replacement for medical or psychiatric care
- A crisis-response resource

Individuals experiencing acute distress, suicidal thoughts, or unsafe situations should contact emergency services or a licensed professional immediately.

How to Use This Workbook

This workbook is designed for:

- Independent recovery work
- Individual therapy
- Group treatment
- Structured recovery programs

Recommended Pace: Complete **one module per week** to allow time for reflection, practice, and integration.

Each module includes:

- Psychoeducation
- Worksheets
- Reflection exercises
- Skills practice
- Behavioral assignments
- Journaling prompts
- Real-world application tasks

Materials Needed

- A journal or notebook
- A private space
- Willingness to be honest
- Commitment to practice

What This Workbook Is Not

This workbook is **not**:

- A replacement for therapy
- A moral or religious text
- A quick fix
- A substitute for medical or psychiatric treatment
- A diagnostic manual

It is a **structured, evidence-based guide** to support your recovery journey.

A Note on Safety and Crisis Resources

If you are experiencing:

- Thoughts of self-harm
- Domestic violence
- Sexual trauma
- Severe emotional distress
- Loss of control over behavior

Seek immediate help from:

- Emergency services
- A licensed mental health professional
- A crisis hotline
- A trusted support person

Your safety comes first.

Introduction

Porn addiction is a behavioral addiction rooted in **neurobiology**, **emotional avoidance**, and **digital reinforcement loops**. It thrives in secrecy, shame, and isolation. Many individuals attempt to quit repeatedly, only to find themselves pulled back into the cycle.

This workbook was created to help you:

- Understand your addiction
- Break the cycle
- Rebuild your identity
- Restore your relationships
- Reclaim your life

You will learn practical skills grounded in:

- Cognitive Behavioral Therapy (CBT)
- Motivational Interviewing (MI)
- Trauma-Informed Care (TIC)
- Emotional regulation
- Relapse-prevention science
- Digital-behavior interventions

Recovery is not about perfection. It is about **progress, honesty, and consistent practice**.

Clinical Orientation

Porn addiction is understood through **five clinical lenses**:

1. Neurobiological

Dopamine, novelty, reinforcement, conditioning.

2. Psychological

Shame, avoidance, emotional dysregulation.

3. Behavioral

Compulsive patterns, triggers, habits, reinforcement loops.

4. Trauma-Informed

Emotional wounds, attachment injuries, survival strategies.

5. Sexual Health

Arousal conditioning, intimacy repair, healthy sexuality.

This workbook integrates all five to create a **comprehensive recovery framework**.

TABLE OF CONTENTS

Front Matter

PART I — FOUNDATIONS OF RECOVERY

PART I — FOUNDATIONS OF RECOVERY

This section establishes the core understanding clients need before they can stabilize, build skills, or engage in deeper recovery work. The tone is clinical, compassionate, and structured — matching your professional voice.

MODULE 1 — UNDERSTANDING PORN ADDICTION

1.0 Purpose of This Module

Clients often arrive confused, ashamed, or unsure whether their behavior "counts" as addiction. This module provides clarity, reduces shame, and establishes a foundation for recovery.

By the end of this module, clients will understand:

- What porn addiction is
- How it develops
- Why it becomes compulsive
- How the cycle operates
- What recovery requires

1.1 What Porn Addiction Is

Porn addiction is a **behavioral addiction** characterized by compulsive engagement with digital sexual content despite negative consequences.

It is defined by:

- Loss of control
- Escalation to more intense or novel content
- Using porn to cope with emotions
- Secrecy or hiding behavior
- Continued use despite harm

It is **not** a moral failure — it is a reinforced behavioral loop that can be changed.

1.2 How Porn Addiction Develops

Neurobiological Factors

Digital sexual content triggers intense dopamine release. Over time, the brain adapts, leading to:

- Tolerance
- Escalation
- Craving
- Compulsive seeking

Emotional Avoidance

Porn becomes a coping strategy for:

- Stress
- Loneliness
- Boredom
- Anxiety
- Conflict
- Emotional overwhelm

Digital Reinforcement

Modern platforms amplify compulsive use through:

- Unlimited novelty
- Instant access
- Privacy
- Algorithmic escalation

Conditioned Arousal

Arousal becomes tied to:

- Specific genres
- Devices
- Times of day
- Rituals
- Emotional states

1.3 The Porn Addiction Cycle

A predictable loop:

1. Emotional discomfort
2. Trigger
3. Rationalization
4. Acting out
5. Temporary relief
6. Shame or regret
7. Avoidance
8. Recommitment
9. Relapse

Understanding the cycle is the first step toward interrupting it.

1.4 Composite Case Example — "Alex"

Alex, 36, used porn to cope with stress and loneliness. He described the cycle as:

"I'd feel stressed, scroll on my phone, tell myself it was harmless, then feel ashamed afterward."

His story reflects the predictable pattern of emotional triggers, digital cues, and conditioned responses.

1.5 Worksheet — Mapping My Cycle

Stage of the Cycle	**My Experience**
Emotional Discomfort	
Triggers	
Rationalization	
Acting Out	
Relief	
Shame/Regret	
Avoidance	
Recommitment	

1.6 Internal & External Triggers

Internal Triggers

- Stress

- Loneliness
- Boredom
- Fatigue
- Anxiety
- Emotional overwhelm

External Triggers

- Privacy
- Late-night scrolling
- Social media
- Certain apps
- Specific locations
- Unstructured time

1.7 Worksheet — Identifying My Triggers

Trigger Type	**Specific Trigger**	**My Example**
Internal		
External		
Digital		

1.8 The Role of Thoughts

Thoughts often act as the "permission slip" for acting out.

Common examples:

- "I deserve this."
- "Just this once."
- "I can handle it."
- "It's not that bad."
- "I'm too stressed to care."

1.9 CBT Worksheet — Thought Awareness Log

Situation	**Automatic Thought**	**New Thought**

1.10 Emotional Avoidance

Porn becomes a coping strategy when clients lack tools to manage:

- Stress
- Conflict
- Rejection
- Shame
- Emotional pain

Recovery requires learning to feel, name, and tolerate emotions.

1.11 Reflection Exercise — What Porn Helps Me Avoid

Prompts:

- "Porn helps me avoid…"……………………………………………………………………………………
- "The emotions I struggle to sit with are…"…………………………………………………………
- "If I didn't use porn to cope, I would need to face…"……………………………………………

1.12 Digital Behavior Patterns

Common patterns include:

- Keeping the phone in bed
- Scrolling late at night
- Using social media as a gateway
- Browsing when bored
- Using devices in private spaces

1.13 Worksheet — My Digital Risk Map

Location	**Risk Level**	**Trigger Example**	**Plan**
Bedroom			
Bathroom			
Car			
Work			

1.14 Grounding Practice

Daily grounding tools:

- 5-4-3-2-1 sensory grounding
- Box breathing
- Temperature change
- Slow exhale breathing
- Movement

1.15 Homework — Early Warning Signs

List 5 signs that indicate you are moving toward relapse.

Examples:

- Increased secrecy
- More time alone
- Avoiding responsibilities
- Emotional numbness
- Late-night scrolling

1.16 Key Takeaways

- Porn addiction is a behavioral addiction
- The cycle is predictable and interruptible
- Triggers are emotional and digital
- Thoughts influence compulsive behavior
- Recovery requires awareness and structure

Homework — My Personal Cycle Narrative

Write a one-page narrative describing your personal addiction cycle in story form. Include:

- What typically triggers the cycle
- How your thoughts justify acting out
- What emotions show up before and after
- What parts of the cycle feel hardest to interrupt
- What you want to change first

MODULE 2 — ASSESSING THE IMPACT OF PORN ADDICTION

2.0 Purpose of This Module

Clients often underestimate the full impact of porn addiction. This module increases insight and reduces minimization.

2.1 Why Assessing Impact Matters

Porn addiction affects:

- Emotions
- Cognition
- Physical health
- Relationships
- Sexual functioning
- Work and responsibilities
- Self-esteem

2.2 Composite Case Example — "Jordan"

Jordan, 29, used porn daily and believed it "wasn't hurting anyone." Over time, he noticed exhaustion, isolation, anxiety, and avoidance.

2.3 Emotional Impact Log

Emotion	Intensity (1–10) Before Porn	After Porn
Shame		
Anxiety		
Loneliness		
Irritability		

2.4 Cognitive Impact Assessment

Cognitive Effect	How It Shows Up	Severity
Preoccupation		
Rationalization		
Distorted Beliefs		
Concentration Issues		

2.5 Physical Impact Log

Physical Effect	Frequency	Severity
Fatigue		
Sleep Problems		

Sexual Issues		
Headaches		

2.6 Relationship Impact Map

Relationship	**Impact**	**Example**	**Notes**
Partner			
Family			
Friends			
Dating			

2.7 Occupational & Daily Functioning

Clients may experience:

- Reduced productivity
- Difficulty focusing
- Procrastination
- Being late or tired
- Avoiding responsibilities

2.8 MI Exercise — Decisional Balance

Staying the Same	**Changing**
Benefits:	Benefits:
Costs:	Costs:

2.9 CBT Homework — Identifying Distortions

Clients list three distorted thoughts related to porn use and rewrite them.

1.
2.
3.

2.10 Emotional Labeling Homework

Clients practice naming emotions daily using a simple list. Use your notebook to keep track of these for 7 days.

2.11 Digital Environment Scan

Location	**Risk Level**	**Trigger Example**	**Plan**
Bedroom			
Bathroom			

Car			
Work			

2.12 Key Takeaways

- Porn addiction affects multiple life domains.
- Awareness increases motivation.
- Minimization decreases with insight.
- Recovery requires addressing emotional, cognitive, physical, and relational areas.

Homework — Impact Reflection Letter

Write a letter to yourself describing the ways porn addiction has affected your:

- Emotions
- Relationships
- Work or school
- Self-esteem
- Daily functioning

End the letter with three reasons you want recovery.

MODULE 3 — UNDERSTANDING TRIGGERS

3.0 Purpose of This Module

Triggers activate cravings and lead to acting out. This module helps clients identify and manage them.

3.1 What Triggers Are

Triggers can be:

- Emotional
- Physical
- Situational
- Digital
- Cognitive
- Relational

Triggers are predictable, not random.

3.2 Composite Case Example — “Luis”

Luis, 41, believed urges “came out of nowhere.” Tracking revealed predictable patterns: stress, loneliness, late-night scrolling, arguments, boredom.

3.3 Internal Trigger Log

Internal Trigger	Emotion	Urge Level
Stress		
Loneliness		
Boredom		
Fatigue		

3.4 External Trigger Map

External Trigger	Location	Plan
Phone in bed	Bedroom	
Social media	Anywhere	
Privacy	Home	

3.5 Digital Trigger Inventory

Digital Trigger	Source	Plan
Social media	Instagram	
Late-night phone	Phone	

Boredom browsing	Laptop	

3.6 Cognitive Trigger Log

Thought	Emotion	Replacement
"Just this once."		
"I deserve this."		
"I can handle it."		

3.7 CBT Homework — Urge Surfing Log

Trigger	Urge Peak (1–10)	Duration

3.8 MI Homework — Change Talk Prompts

Prompts:

- "I want to change because..."
- "My life would improve if..."
- "I'm tired of..."

3.9 Trauma-Informed Safety Plan

Clients list grounding strategies for high-risk moments:

- Breathing
- Sensory grounding
- Movement
- Calling someone
- Leaving the environment

3.10 High-Risk Map

High-Risk Situation	**Why It's Risky**	**My Plan**

3.11 Digital Trigger Removal Plan

Trigger	**Digital Source**	**Removal Plan**

3.12 Key Takeaways

- Triggers are predictable
- Awareness reduces impulsivity
- Managing triggers is essential for relapse prevention
- Digital triggers require specific strategies

- Thoughts, emotions, and environments all influence urges

Homework — 48-Hour Trigger Journal

For the next two days, track every moment you notice:

- A trigger
- A shift in emotion
- A thought that increases risk
- A digital cue

Record:

1. What happened
2. What you felt
3. What you did
4. What you wish you had done

PART II — STABILIZATION & SKILLS

Part II equips clients with the core skills needed to interrupt compulsive behavior, manage urges, rebuild sexual health, and create a sustainable recovery plan. These modules shift clients from *understanding* their addiction to *actively changing* their patterns.

MODULE 4 — MANAGING CRAVINGS & URGES

4.0 Purpose of This Module

Cravings and urges are a normal part of recovery. This module teaches clients how to:

- Understand cravings
- Identify urge patterns
- Interrupt the urge cycle
- Use CBT and mindfulness tools
- Build a personalized craving-management plan

The goal is not to eliminate urges but to respond skillfully.

4.1 What Cravings Are

Cravings are intense internal experiences that create pressure to act out. They may include:

- Physical sensations
- Emotional discomfort
- Mental images
- Sexual arousal
- Restlessness
- Impulsive thoughts

Cravings are **temporary, predictable, and manageable**.

4.2 The Urge Wave

Urges rise, peak, and fall like a wave. Most urges last **5–20 minutes** when not acted upon.

Clients often believe urges will grow stronger until they "explode," but this is a distortion. The urge wave always subsides.

4.3 Composite Case Example — "Ethan"

Ethan, 32, believed his urges were "too strong to resist." When he tracked them, he discovered:

- Urges peaked quickly
- They faded within minutes
- Distraction helped
- Breathing reduced intensity

He said, "Once I learned to ride the wave, the urge lost its power."

4.4 Components of an Urge

Urges often include:

- **Thoughts:** "I need this."
- **Emotions:** stress, loneliness, boredom
- **Sensations:** tightness, restlessness
- **Images:** sexual memories or fantasies
- **Impulses:** reaching for the phone

Understanding these components helps clients intervene earlier.

4.5 Worksheet — My Urge Profile

Component	**My Experience**	**Notes**
Thoughts		

Emotions		
Sensations		
Images		
Impulses		

4.6 CBT Tool — Urge Surfing

Urge surfing teaches clients to:

- Notice the urge
- Observe it without judgment
- Breathe through discomfort
- Allow the urge to rise and fall
- Stay present until it passes

This reduces impulsivity and increases emotional tolerance.

4.7 Worksheet — Urge Surfing Log

Trigger	Urge Peak (1–10)	Duration

4.8 MI Tool — Strengthening Commitment

Prompts:

- "I want to resist urges because…"
- "My life improves when I stay committed by…"
- "I'm capable of managing urges because…"

4.9 Trauma-Informed Grounding

Clients' practice:

- Slow exhale breathing
- Sensory grounding
- Temperature change
- Movement
- Naming emotions

These reduce overwhelm and increase control.

4.10 Digital Delay & Disrupt Tools

Clients practice delaying access to devices by:

- Moving the phone to another room
- Using timers
- Standing up and walking
- Changing posture
- Interrupting the ritual

4.11 Worksheet — My Craving-Management Plan

Strategy	**When I'll Use It**	**Notes**
Delay		
Breathing		
Movement		
Distraction		
Calling Someone		

4.12 Key Takeaways

- Urges are temporary
- Urges follow a predictable wave pattern
- Skills reduce the intensity of cravings
- Clients can learn to respond instead of reacting

Homework — Urge Practice Drill

Choose one urge-management skill (breathing, grounding, delay, movement). For the next three days, practice it **once per day, even without an urge**. Document:

- Which skill do you practice
- How long have you practiced
- What you noticed in your body
- How confident do you feel using it during real urges

MODULE 5 — REBUILDING SEXUAL HEALTH & INTIMACY

5.0 Purpose of This Module

Porn addiction affects sexual functioning, intimacy, and relational connection. This module helps clients:

- Understand the impact of porn on sexuality
- Rebuild healthy arousal patterns
- Strengthen emotional intimacy
- Reduce shame
- Develop a healthier sexual identity

5.1 How Porn Affects Sexual Health

Porn addiction can influence:

- Arousal patterns
- Sexual expectations
- Performance
- Desire
- Connection
- Body image
- Confidence

Clients may experience:

- Delayed arousal

- Erectile difficulties
- Reduced sensitivity
- Performance anxiety
- Difficulty connecting emotionally

5.2 Composite Case Example — "Marcus"

Marcus, 38, reported:

- Difficulty becoming aroused with partners
- Feeling disconnected during sex
- Needing specific porn content to feel stimulated
- Feeling ashamed about his preferences

He said, "I didn't realize porn had rewired what I found arousing."

5.3 Reconditioning Arousal

Clients learn to:

- Reduce porn exposure
- Rebuild sensitivity
- Shift arousal toward real connection
- Practice mindful arousal
- Reduce performance pressure

5.4 Worksheet — Sexual Health Inventory

Area	Current Experience	Goal
Arousal		
Desire		
Confidence		
Connection		

5.5 Emotional Intimacy

Clients often struggle with:

- Vulnerability
- Trust
- Communication
- Presence
- Emotional availability

Porn becomes a substitute for intimacy, not a supplement.

5.6 Communication Skills

Clients' practice:

- Naming needs
- Expressing boundaries

- Repairing ruptures
- Listening with presence

5.7 Shame Reduction Work

Clients explore:

- Sources of shame
- Internalized messages
- Self-compassion practices
- Healthy sexual identity

5.8 Partner-Oriented Healing

For partnered clients:

- Transparency
- Rebuilding trust
- Collaborative healing
- Shared boundaries

5.9 Key Takeaways

- Porn impacts sexual health and intimacy
- Arousal can be reconditioned
- Emotional intimacy is a skill
- Shame reduction is essential for healing

Homework — Healthy Sexuality Reflection

Write a reflection answering:

- What does healthy sexuality mean to me?
- How has porn shaped my expectations?
- What do I want intimacy to look like in the future?
- What fears or insecurities show up around sexual connection?

MODULE 6 — BUILDING A SUSTAINABLE RECOVERY PLAN

6.0 Purpose of This Module

Clients need a structured, sustainable plan to maintain progress. This module helps them build routines, boundaries, and accountability systems.

6.1 Daily Structure & Routines

Clients create:

- Morning routines
- Evening routines
- Device boundaries
- Self-care practices
- Emotional check-ins

Consistency builds stability.

6.2 Accountability Systems

Clients identify:

- Support people
- Check-in routines
- Recovery partners
- Therapy or group support
- Digital accountability tools

Accountability increases follow-through.

6.3 Digital Boundaries

Clients set:

- Device-free zones
- Screen-time limits
- Content filters
- Social media boundaries
- Nighttime device rules

6.4 Relapse-Prevention Basics

Clients learn:

- Early warning signs
- High-risk situations
- Coping strategies
- Emergency plans

6.5 Worksheet — My Recovery Plan

Area	**My Plan**	**Notes**
Daily Routine		
Accountability		
Digital Boundaries		

Coping Skills		
Support People		

6.6 Key Takeaways

- Recovery requires structure
- Accountability increases success
- Digital boundaries protect progress
- A personalized plan supports long-term change

Homework — 7-Day Micro-Routine Challenge

Choose **one** small daily habit that supports recovery (e.g., a morning check-in, a device-free hour, or journaling). Practice it for **seven consecutive days**. Track:

- Whether you completed it
- What helped
- What got in the way
- How it affected your urges or mood

PART III — DEEP RECOVERY WORK

Part III moves clients beyond stabilization into the deeper psychological and emotional layers that sustain long-term recovery. These modules help clients rebuild identity, heal emotional wounds, and create a new personal narrative.

MODULE 7 — IDENTITY, VALUES & THE SELF

7.0 Purpose of This Module

Porn addiction often disconnects clients from their identity, values, and sense of self. This module helps clients:

- Reconnect with who they are
- Clarify what matters most
- Reduce shame
- Build a value-driven recovery

7.1 Identity Reconstruction

Clients explore:

- Who they were before addiction
- Who they became during addiction
- Who they want to become in recovery

Prompts:

- "My addiction made me feel like..."
- "The version of me I miss is..."
- "The version of me I want to become is..."

Identity shifts from shame-based to value-based.

7.2 Values Clarification

Values guide behavior and shape recovery.

Common values include:

- Integrity
- Family
- Faith
- Health
- Growth
- Connection
- Honesty
- Responsibility

Clients identify their top five values.

7.3 Shame Reduction

Shame fuels secrecy and relapse. Clients learn:

- The difference between guilt and shame
- How shame distorts identity
- How to practice self-compassion
- How to challenge shame-based beliefs

7.4 Worksheet — Values Inventory

Value	**Why It Matters to Me**	**How I Will Live It**
Integrity		
Family		
Health		

Growth			
Connection			

7.5 Key Takeaways

- Identity can be rebuilt
- Values guide recovery
- Shame decreases when clients reconnect with their true selves

Homework — Values in Action Plan

Select your top two values. For each value, list:

- One behavior you will start
- One behavior you will stop
- One boundary you will set
- One way you will live this value this week

MODULE 8 — HEALING EMOTIONAL WOUNDS

8.0 Purpose of This Module

Porn addiction often develops as a coping strategy for unresolved emotional pain. This module helps clients:

- Understand emotional wounds
- Build emotional regulation skills
- Explore attachment patterns
- Develop healthier coping strategies

8.1 Trauma-Informed Framework

Clients learn:

- Trauma does not always mean "big events"
- Emotional wounds can come from neglect, rejection, or chronic stress
- Porn becomes a survival strategy
- Healing requires safety, compassion, and patience

8.2 Emotional Regulation Skills

Clients practice:

- Naming emotions
- Tolerating discomfort
- Using grounding tools
- Practicing self-soothing
- Reducing emotional avoidance

Skills include:

- Box breathing
- 5-4-3-2-1 grounding
- Progressive relaxation
- Urge surfing
- Journaling

8.3 Attachment Patterns

Clients explore how attachment influences:

- Intimacy
- Trust
- Emotional availability
- Conflict
- Coping strategies

Common patterns:

- Avoidant
- Anxious
- Disorganized
- Secure

Clients identify their primary pattern.

8.4 Worksheet — Emotional Wounds Map

Emotional Wound	How It Shows Up Today	Healthy Response Plan
Rejection		
Abandonment		
Shame		
Criticism		

8.5 Key Takeaways

- Emotional wounds influence addiction
- Emotional regulation reduces compulsive behavior
- Attachment patterns shape intimacy and coping
- Healing is possible with awareness and practice

Homework — Emotional Regulation Practice Log

Choose one emotional regulation skill from this module. Use it **three times** this week when you feel discomfort. Record:

- What emotion you felt
- What skill you used
- How effective it was
- What you learned about yourself

MODULE 9 — REWRITING YOUR STORY

9.0 Purpose of This Module

Clients often carry a story shaped by shame, failure, or hopelessness. This module helps them rewrite their narrative with honesty, compassion, and purpose.

9.1 Narrative Reconstruction

Clients explore:

- The story they've been living
- The beliefs they've internalized
- The messages they've absorbed
- The identity they've carried

Prompts:

- "The story I've been telling myself is…"
- "This story has affected me by…"
- "This story is incomplete because…"

9.2 Meaning-Making

Clients learn to:

- Extract meaning from struggle
- Identify lessons
- Recognize resilience
- Reframe setbacks

- Build a hopeful narrative

9.3 Future Identity Work

Clients define:

- Who they want to become
- What habits support that identity
- What boundaries protect that identity
- What relationships reinforce that identity

9.4 Worksheet — My New Story

| **Old Story (1–2 sentences)** |

| **New Story (1–2 sentences)** |

| **Habits That Support My New Story** |

| **Boundaries That Protect My New Story** |

| **People Who Support My New Story** |

9.5 Key Takeaways

- Clients can rewrite their story.

- Meaning-making strengthens recovery.
- Identity shifts create long-term change.

Homework — Future Self Letter

Write a letter from your **future self (1 year into recovery)** to your current self. Include:

- What your life looks like
- How you feel about yourself
- What habits helped you get there?
- What you want your current self to know

PART IV — LONG-TERM RECOVERY & LIFESTYLE TRANSFORMATION

Part IV prepares clients for the long-term journey. By this stage, they have stabilized, built skills, and begun deeper emotional work. Now they learn how to:

- Prevent relapses!
- Build healthy sexuality!
- Transform their lifestyle!
- Maintain long-term growth!

These modules shift clients from *recovery* to *transformation*.

MODULE 10 — ADVANCED RELAPSE PREVENTION

10.0 Purpose of This Module

Relapse prevention is not about perfection — it is about **pattern recognition**, **early intervention**, and **long-term strategy**.

This module helps clients:

- Understand relapse patterns
- Identify early warning signs
- Build advanced prevention strategies
- Strengthen long-term resilience

10.1 Relapse Patterns

Relapses are a **process**, not an event.

Common patterns:

- Emotional buildup
- Isolation
- Avoidance
- Increased secrecy
- Digital drift
- Rationalization
- "Mini-relapses" (gateway behaviors)

Clients learn to identify their personal patterns.

10.2 Early Warning Signs

Examples include:

- Increased irritability
- Emotional numbness
- Avoiding responsibilities
- Staying up late
- Scrolling without purpose
- Hiding device use
- Feeling disconnected

Clients list their top five warning signs.

10.3 Long-Term Strategies

Clients develop:

- Emotional regulation routines
- Accountability systems
- Digital boundaries
- Healthy coping skills
- Structured daily habits
- Relapse-response plans

10.4 Worksheet — Relapse Prevention Map

Warning Sign	**What It Means for Me**	**My Response Plan**

10.5 Key Takeaways

- Relapses are predictable
- Early warning signs matter
- Long-term strategies protect progress
- Clients can recover quickly from setbacks

Homework — Relapse Simulation Exercise

Imagine a realistic high-risk situation. Write out:

1. What would the trigger be?
2. What thoughts might show up?
3. What emotions would you feel?
4. What would your relapse-prevention plan be?
5. What would you do in the first 10 minutes?

MODULE 11 — HEALTHY SEXUALITY & RELATIONSHIPS

11.0 Purpose of This Module

Porn addiction distorts sexual expectations, intimacy, and relational connection. This module helps clients:

- Rebuild healthy sexual scripts.
- Strengthen intimacy.
- Repair relationships
- Develop a healthy sexual identity.

11.1 Healthy Sexual Scripts

Clients explore:

- What healthy sexuality looks like
- How porn shaped their expectations
- How to rebuild realistic, connected sexual experiences

Healthy sexuality includes:

- Consent
- Connection
- Presence
- Mutual pleasure
- Emotional safety

11.2 Intimacy Skills

Clients' practice:

- Vulnerability
- Emotional presence
- Communication
- Attunement
- Repairing ruptures

Intimacy is a skill, not a personality trait.

11.3 Relationship Repair

Clients learn:

- How to rebuild trust
- How to communicate transparently
- How to set boundaries
- How to repair after conflict
- How to reconnect emotionally

For partnered clients, this section can be done individually or with a therapist.

11.4 Worksheet — Relationship Health Inventory

Area of Relationship	**Current Status**	**Goal**
Communication		
Trust		

Emotional Intimacy		
Sexual Connection		

11.5 Key Takeaways

- Healthy sexuality is learned.
- Intimacy requires presence and vulnerability.
- Relationships can heal with honesty and effort.

Homework — Relationship Repair Micro-Steps

Identify **one** relationship you want to strengthen. List three small actions you can take this week to improve:

- Communication
- Trust
- Emotional presence

MODULE 12 — LIFESTYLE TRANSFORMATION & LONG-TERM GROWTH

12.0 Purpose of This Module

Recovery is not just about stopping porn — it's about building a meaningful, connected, purpose-driven life.

This module helps clients:

- Build healthy habits.
- Strengthen purpose.
- Maintain long-term growth.
- Create a lifestyle that supports freedom.

12.1 Habits & Routines

Clients develop:

- Morning routines
- Evening routines
- Emotional check-ins
- Movement practices
- Digital hygiene
- Sleep routines

Habits create stability and reduce vulnerability.

12.2 Purpose & Meaning

Clients explore:

- What gives their life meaning?
- What they want to contribute
- How they want to grow
- What kind of person do they want to become?

Prompts:

- "My life feels meaningful when…"
- "I feel most alive when…"
- "I want to grow in the direction of…"

12.3 Long-Term Maintenance

Clients learn:

- How to maintain progress
- How to respond to setbacks
- How to stay connected
- How to continue emotional work
- How to protect their identity

12.4 Worksheet — Lifestyle Transformation Plan

Area	**My Plan**	**Notes**
Health		
Relationships		

Purpose			
Habits			
Digital Life			

12.5 Key Takeaways

- Recovery becomes transformation.
- Habits shape identity.
- Purpose strengthens long-term freedom.
- Clients can build a life they are proud of

Homework — 30-Day Freedom Blueprint

Create a one-page plan outlining:

- Three habits you will build.
- Three habits you will eliminate.
- Three boundaries you will maintain.
- Three people or communities you will stay connected to
- Three goals for the next 30 days

PART V — LIVING IN FREEDOM

Part V is the culmination of the entire workbook. It shifts clients from:

- “I’m trying to stop porn” to
- “I’m building a meaningful, connected, purpose-driven life.”

This section reinforces long-term identity, community, and the mindset needed to sustain freedom.

LIFE AFTER ADDICTION

Purpose of This Section

Clients often fear that recovery will always feel like a battle. This section reframes long-term recovery as:

- A lifestyle
- A mindset
- A set of habits
- A way of relating to oneself and others
- A commitment to growth

Freedom is not the absence of urges — it is the presence of purpose, structure, and connection.

What Long-Term Freedom Looks Like

Client's experience:

- Increased emotional stability
- Stronger relationships
- Healthier sexuality
- Improved self-esteem
- Greater confidence
- More energy
- Clearer thinking
- A sense of purpose

Freedom is not perfection — it is resilience.

The Shift from Avoidance to Engagement

Clients move from:

- Avoiding triggers
- Avoiding emotions
- Avoiding intimacy
- Avoiding responsibility

to:

- Engaging with life
- Engaging with relationships
- Engaging with purpose
- Engaging with growth

This shift is the foundation of long-term transformation.

Worksheets - My Life After Addiction

Area of Life	**What Freedom Looks Like for Me**	**First Steps**
Emotional Health		
Relationships		
Sexual Health		
Purpose		
Daily Habits		

COMMUNITY, CONNECTION & SUPPORT

Why Community Matters

Addiction thrives in isolation. Recovery thrives in connection.

Clients learn that:

- Support reduces relapse
- Connection increases accountability
- Community reduces shame
- Relationships provide meaning
- Vulnerability builds strength

No one recovers alone.

Types of Support

Clients identify:

- Trusted friends
- Family members
- Support groups
- Therapists
- Faith communities
- Recovery partners
- Mentors

Support is not a sign of weakness — it is a sign of wisdom.

Building a Support Network

Clients create a simple, actionable plan:

1. Identify 3 people you can reach out to

2. Identify 3 people you want to build deeper connection with

3. Identify 3 communities you want to explore

Worksheet — My Support Network

Person/Group	How They Support Me	How I Will Stay Connected

BECOMING THE PERSON YOU WERE MEANT TO BE

Purpose of This Section

This final section helps clients step into a new identity — one shaped by:

- Integrity
- Purpose
- Connection
- Growth
- Self-respect

Recovery is not about becoming someone new — it is about returning to who they truly are.

Identity in Freedom

Clients explore:

- Who they are becoming
- What they value
- How they want to show up
- What kind of partner, friend, or parent they want to be
- What kind of life they want to build

Prompts:

- "The person I am becoming is..."
- "I want to be known as someone who..."
- "My life will reflect my values by..."

The Freedom Mindset

Clients adopt a mindset of:

- Growth
- Curiosity
- Compassion
- Accountability
- Purpose
- Resilience

Freedom is not the absence of struggle — it is the presence of strength.

Worksheet — My Freedom Identity Statement

My Freedom Identity (2–3 sentences)
Habits That Support This Identity
Boundaries That Protect This Identity
Relationships That Reinforce This Identity

Closing Reflection

Clients reflect on:

- How far they've come
- What they've learned
- Who they have become

- What they want to continue building

Prompts:

- "The biggest change I've made is..."
- "The part of myself I'm most proud of is..."
- "The life I'm building now includes..."

CONCLUSION

Recovery from porn addiction is not a straight line. It is a journey of honesty, courage, and consistent practice. You have worked through twelve modules that challenged you to:

- Understand your addiction
- Build emotional awareness
- Strengthen coping skills
- Heal emotional wounds
- Rebuild identity
- Repair relationships
- Create a meaningful life
- Step into long-term freedom

You have done the hard work of looking inward — and that is something to be proud of.

As you move forward, remember:

- You are not defined by your past
- You are capable of change
- You are worthy of connection
- You can build a life that reflects your values
- You can continue growing long after this workbook ends

Recovery is not about perfection. It is about resilience, honesty, and choosing growth one day at a time.

You have already proven you can do hard things. Now continue building the life you were meant to live.

ACKNOWLEDGMENTS

To every client who has trusted me with their story — thank you. Your courage, honesty, and resilience inspired the creation of this workbook.

To the individuals and families impacted by compulsive pornography use — your healing matters. Your willingness to seek help is a powerful act of strength.

To the clinicians, mentors, and colleagues who continue to advance the field of behavioral addiction treatment — your dedication makes recovery possible for countless individuals.

And to my family — thank you for your support, patience, and belief in the work I do. Your encouragement fuels my commitment to helping others find freedom.

ABOUT THE AUTHOR

James Martinez, MS, LCADC, LSATP, CAADC, CASAC-II, CCS, ICGC Licensed Addiction Therapist Founder, Stress Free Recovery LLC

James Martinez is a nationally credentialed addiction specialist with over 15 years of clinical experience treating behavioral addictions, including gambling addiction, compulsive pornography use, and compulsive sexual behavior. He is the creator of multiple evidence-based clinical workbooks used by individuals, therapists, and recovery programs across the United States.

His work integrates:

- Cognitive Behavioral Therapy (CBT)
- Motivational Interviewing (MI)
- Trauma-Informed Care (TIC)
- Emotional regulation
- Relapse-prevention science
- Culturally responsive treatment

itself is qualitatively wrong for any age, by comparing the observed pattern against the full developmental sequence rather than against a single age-expected snapshot; a pattern that matches the expected appearance of a younger age is more likely delayed myelination, often associated with a nonspecific global developmental delay, whereas a pattern that does not correspond to any normal age, such as an unusual, patchy, or asymmetric signal distribution, is more concerning for a primary white matter disease and warrants the leukodystrophy evaluation detailed in Chapter 17.

Approximate Age	Structures With Adult-Pattern T1 Signal	Structures With Adult-Pattern T2 Signal
Term neonate	Brainstem, posterior limb internal capsule, ventrolateral thalamus	Brainstem, posterior limb internal capsule
6 months	Most central white matter, cerebellar white matter	Central white matter beginning to mature
12 months	Nearly adult pattern throughout	Central and paracentral white matter
18–24 months	Fully adult pattern	Nearly adult pattern; peripheral frontal/temporal white matter matures last

Myelination Assessment Using Standardized Age Charts

Standardized myelination charts, mapping the expected T1 and T2 appearance of specific anatomic landmarks against age in months, provide a more reproducible assessment than global visual impression alone and are particularly useful when the clinical question is specifically whether myelination is age-appropriate, as in the evaluation of global developmental delay; using a small, consistent set of landmark structures, including the posterior limb of the internal capsule, the splenium of the corpus callosum, and the peripheral centrum semiovale, rather than attempting to assess the entire brain simultaneously, improves both the speed and the reproducibility of this determination.

Common Referral Question: Is This Child's Myelination Normal?

This precise question, generated most often by a developmental pediatrician evaluating a child with global developmental delay, is best answered systematically rather than impressionistically: the interpreting clinician confirms the child's exact corrected age, checks the small set of landmark structures named above against the standardized age chart, and states explicitly in the report whether the pattern observed matches the child's chronologic age, matches a younger age consistent with delayed but qualitatively normal myelination, or fails to match any normal age at all; this last category, rather than the first two, is the pattern that should prompt the leukodystrophy and metabolic evaluation detailed in Chapter 17.

A report that states only myelination appears delayed, without specifying which landmark structures were assessed or what corrected age the pattern actually corresponds to, gives the referring developmental pediatrician far less to act on than a report stating specifically that myelination corresponds to an approximately twelve-month pattern in a child chronologically aged twenty-four months, a formulation that allows the referring clinician to weigh the degree of delay directly against the child's broader developmental trajectory rather than working from a vague qualitative impression alone.

THE CLINICAL-IMAGING CROSSWALK SYSTEM — A Neonate Referred for 'Delayed' Myelination on an Outside Report

---

The Crossing: A term neonate undergoes brain MRI for a mildly abnormal newborn examination, and the outside report describes the white matter as showing delayed myelination for age.

Presentation Signature: A term-born infant with an otherwise unremarkable, nonfocal examination, referred specifically because the imaging report used the phrase delayed myelination without further qualification.

Imaging Correlate: Review of the actual images against the age-expected timeline confirms T1 hyperintensity appropriately present in the brainstem, posterior limb of the internal capsule, and ventrolateral thalamus, exactly as expected at term, with the remaining cerebral white matter appropriately unmyelinated for a neonate; the outside interpretation reflects a misunderstanding of the normal term appearance, not a true finding.

Trap Logic: A term neonate's cerebral white matter is expected to appear largely unmyelinated; describing this normal, expected pattern as delayed myelination, rather than as an age-appropriate finding, generates unwarranted parental anxiety and inappropriate referral for a nonexistent problem.

Crossing Anchor: Myelination status must always be interpreted against the specific structures expected to be myelinated at the child's exact corrected age, never against a generic adult-pattern expectation regardless of age.

Normal Variants of the Skull, Ventricles, and Posterior Fossa

A substantial fraction of pediatric neuroimaging referrals for an incidental finding trace back to one of a small number of well-characterized normal anatomic variants, each of which has a distinctive, learnable appearance that distinguishes it from a genuinely pathologic process. Recognizing these variants confidently is one of the highest-yield skills this book teaches, because failing to recognize them generates unnecessary follow-up imaging, unnecessary specialist referral, and unwarranted family anxiety.

Benign Enlargement of the Subarachnoid Spaces

Benign enlargement of the subarachnoid spaces of infancy, most prominent over the frontal convexities, presents typically between three and eighteen months of age, is frequently associated with macrocephaly that tracks along a growth curve parallel to but above the standard percentile lines, and is distinguished from pathologic extra-axial fluid collections, including chronic subdural hemorrhage, by the absence of membranes, the presence of visible, uncompressed cortical veins traversing the fluid space, and a